FASTBACK® Mystery

Bill Waite's Will

ALLAN MOORE

GLOBE FEARON
Pearson Learning Group

FASTBACK® MYSTERY BOOKS

Bill Waite's Will
Cardiac Arrest
Dawson's City
The Diary
The Face That Stopped Time
A Game for Fools

The Good Luck Smiling Cat
The Intruder
Janie
Meeting at Joe's
No Witnesses
Suspicion

All photography © Pearson Education, Inc. (PEI) unless specifically noted.

Copyright © 2004 by Pearson Education, Inc., publishing as Globe Fearon®, an imprint of Pearson Learning Group, 299 Jefferson Road, Parsippany, NJ 07054. All rights reserved. No part of this book may be reproduced or transmitted in any form or by any means, electronic or mechanical, including photocopying, recording, or by any information storage and retrieval system, without permission in writing from the publisher. For information regarding permission(s), write to Rights and Permissions Department.

Globe Fearon® and Fastback® are registered trademarks of Globe Fearon, Inc.

ISBN 0-13-024537-2
Printed in the United States of America
1 2 3 4 5 6 7 8 9 10   07 06 05 04 03

1-800-321-3106
www.pearsonlearning.com

Cally Enright looked down at the town in the valley. Pushing his hat back, he wiped his face with an old bandana. So that was Red Rock. Not much of a place.

"A man could walk right by it in the night," he said aloud to Juliet. The mule swished her tail. She bent her head to chew on the brown desert grass.

The afternoon air was dry and hot. The sun burned in the clear blue sky. Flies buzzed around Cally and the old mule as they stood on the rise. At last, Cally licked his cracked lips and pulled on the rope. "C'mon, Juliet," he said. "Let's go down there and take care of business."

Cally was short. His face was covered by a rough, gray beard. The few teeth he had were crooked. His eyes were the color of a summer sky, and the corners were creased into hundreds of tiny wrinkles. He wore an old hat to shade his eyes from the hurting sun. His shirt, pants, and boots were covered with dirt from the mountains. Until two days ago, he had been digging for gold. But today was different—he had business to take care of.

And he needed a drink! His throat was burning from the hot desert air.

Down in the valley, Cally made his way through the small desert town. He went past ugly, unpainted houses with missing boards. The streets were empty. Nothing moved in the midday heat except a buzzard high in the still air. It made lazy circles in the blue sky.

Cally stopped in front of the first saloon, licking his lips. He tied up the mule and went inside.

"Howdy," someone said.

Cally nodded his head. "Howdy." At first he couldn't see in the sudden darkness of the room. Then he saw the man behind the bar and smiled at him. "Howdy, friend," Cally said.

"What will you have, old-timer?" the bartender asked.

"Beer," Cally said, slapping a coin

down on the bar. He smiled as the glass was put before him. Oh! He was thirsty! He drank the beer right down and waved for another.

As the bartender gave the second beer to Cally, he asked, "You bring any news?"

Cally shook his head. "I came from up in the hills."

He looked around. He saw that he was in a long room with tables and a piano. Behind the bar were stacks of glasses and a large mirror. The bartender left Cally with his beer and went back to the end of the bar to look out into the street.

Three other men were in the room. Two of them were playing cards at a back table. One was standing near Cally at the bar. Cally took his glass and moved closer to the stranger.

"Howdy," he said. "My name's Cally Enright. I'm from up in the hills. Is there any law here?"

The man turned, and his gray eyes studied Cally. He was dressed as a cowhand, checked shirt and jeans. Then Cally saw the silver star pinned to the shirt. The man smiled.

"Hello, Cally," the man said. "I'm Jeff Fraser." He put out his hand. "What do you want law for?" he asked.

Cally shook hands with him. Fraser had a square, honest face with a heavy shadow along his jaw. His badge read "Deputy Sheriff." Cally fished in his pocket and brought out a folded paper.

"I got a will here, Mr. Fraser. Last will and testament." He put it back in his pocket.

Fraser asked, "Is that your will?"

"No. My partner, Bill Waite, died a few days ago up in the hills. Fever got him. Old Bill and me were partners for 10 years. We came down here to find a claim about a year back."

The deputy nodded.

Cally said, "I thought I better get the will recorded so I could stay and work the claim. I want it all legal."

"All right, Cally." Fraser rubbed his nose. "That's out of my line, but the sheriff will be in town in the morning. I reckon he'll know what to do. Your claim is across the creek?"

"A couple of days' ride south. Me and Bill used to go over to South Fork for supplies, but there's no law there." Cally drank his last gulp of beer.

"Donovan," Fraser called. "Get another beer for my friend Cally."

"Why, thanks, Mr. Fraser."

The bartender brought Cally the beer and went back to staring out the window. The deputy asked, "Are you fixing to stay long, Cally?"

Cally shook his head. "I got to get back soon as I can. I got just three dollars in hard money." He smiled. "It'll be getting cold, too, pretty soon. I have to fix the roof on the shack."

Fraser said, "There's no hotel in town. But you go over to the livery and tell Jonas that I sent you. He'll let you sleep in one of the stalls."

"I sure thank you, Mr. Fraser."

The deputy smiled, nodded to Donovan, and walked out.

Cally finished his beer slowly. Then he set the glass down and went out with a wave to Donovan. The bartender nodded to him.

Outside Cally made his way up the dusty street. He led Juliet behind him. Cally was glad that he had come to town. Juliet was company, but not much for conversation.

He found the livery stable at the end of the main street. It was a large building with a corral at the side. A big man sat just inside the open door. Cally figured that the man must be Jonas. He was huge, with dirty black hair, no neck, and heavy shoulders. And he was asleep. A newspaper slipped from his hands as he snored loudly.

Cally left Juliet in the shade of the building. Then he took off his hat and slapped it against his leg. Jonas opened his eyes.

"Hello, Mr. Jonas," Cally said. "My name is Cally Enright. Deputy Fraser said maybe you'd let me bed down in an empty stall if you had one. I won't be any trouble, and I'm willing to pay."

Jonas looked him over. "I got one," he said at last in a deep voice. "Feed for the mule will cost you, though. I'm not running a hotel."

"Sure," Cally agreed. He rattled the coins in his pocket.

Jonas stood and stretched. "Come on in out of the heat."

Cally followed the big man inside where the air was slightly cooler. The smells of animals and fresh hay hung in the air. Cally sighed. This wasn't much like the hot, dusty rocks of the canyon where the claim was.

"You can put your stuff in that stall," Jonas said, pointing. "There's water out back."

"Mighty friendly of you, Jonas." Cally led Juliet into the stall and began to struggle with the knots on the dusty pack.

"You play gin rummy?" demanded the big man.

Cally grinned and nodded. "Sure do."

Cally washed his clothes in a bucket behind the stable. Soon the day had faded into evening. The angry sun was gone behind the faraway mountains. The air seemed less dry. A soft, cool breeze made its way through the town. People came to their doors and sat in chairs on their porches. Yellow lights came on in the saloons along Front Street. Cally heard the pianos playing and the sounds of people talking. The town had come alive.

Cally smiled. He sure felt good being with people again. He put out his little cooking fire and covered it with dirt. He had the livery to himself now. Jonas had gone home for a bit and had left him in charge. Cally lit a lamp and hung it by the door. He talked to Juliet a moment and filled his pipe. Not much tobacco left. He would have to stock up at the store tomorrow before he went back.

With the pipe going well, Cally pulled out the will and unfolded it. He knew it by heart. It was only a few lines written on the back of an old poster. Bill Waite had insisted on writing it himself. By the lamp's light, Cally read the will once more.

LAST WILL AND TESTAMENT
To whom it may concern. I, Bill Waite, being of sound mind and going to die of fever, hereby leave everything I own to my partner, Cally Enright. This means my half of the claim and my gun.

Bill Waite

The signature made Cally smile. Old Bill had signed his name with fancy big loops. But then the smile left Cally's face. He remembered the grave on the lonely hillside. The picture stayed in his mind until he got up and went to work with a rake.

When he finished, he sat in Jonas's stool by the door and waited for the big man to return.

Cally listened to the sounds of the night. After a while someone passed by, walking his horse slowly. Then Cally heard a greeting called from the darkness. A moment later, Jonas came into the circle of light. He went on into the stable and returned with a deck of old cards. They cut for deal.

They played gin rummy for the better part of an hour. Near nine o'clock Jonas pulled out his big watch, clicked the lid open, and looked at Cally. "It's getting late," Jonas said.

Cally nodded. He gathered up the cards. They took a last look at the sky and turned in.

In the morning, Cally walked to the sheriff's office. It was a low building made of stones, with two small, barred windows facing the street. Inside the office Deputy Fraser was sitting in a chair tilted back against the wall. He grinned as Cally entered.

"Howdy, Cally," Fraser said. "Did Jonas treat you right?"

"He sure did, Mr. Fraser. Thanks. Jonas

is just fine." Cally looked around. "Is the sheriff here?"

"He's out back, washing up. He'll be here in a minute."

Cally dropped onto a hard bench and looked through the small window. "Looks like it'll be hot again today."

The back door opened just then and the sheriff entered, wiping his hands on a towel. He was a very tall man with stringy, almost gray hair. He wore a black tie and a faded blue shirt. Seeing Cally, he said, "Morning." His black eyebrows made a nearly straight line across his tanned face—except where one brow was broken by a small scar.

Cally stared at the man, gasped, and slid off the bench. "You . . . you're the sheriff?"

The other man nodded and dropped the towel onto a chair, his eyes on Cally.

"This is Sheriff Roy Thomas," Fraser said. He went over and slapped Cally on the back. "Roy, this here is Cally Enright. He wants to see you about a will."

The sheriff stared at Cally. "That so?"

"His partner died up in the hills," Fraser went on. "Cally just wants the claim to be legal and all. I told him—"

"I was just stringing you along," Cally said quickly. He edged toward the door, shaking off the deputy's arm. He laughed nervously, his eyes on the sheriff. "It's not important."

Fraser swung around in surprise. "What's got into you?"

Cally grabbed at the door handle. "Nothing to bother you about."

Sheriff Thomas took a step and held out his hand. "Let me see that will."

Cally said, "I haven't got it . . . I mean, I forgot it." He tugged at the door.

"What's wrong with you, Cally?" Fraser stepped toward him. "Are you all right?"

Cally tried to smile but couldn't. The door opened with a jerk. "Don't bother about me," Cally said. He looked back quickly at the sheriff, his eyes like those of a cornered animal. Then he slid through the door and slammed it shut.

Cally ran along the boardwalk. The sun seemed to beat into his brain. He looked over his shoulder, but no one had come out of the sheriff's office. Hurrying on, he got his breath back by the time he reached the stable.

Jonas was surprised when Cally rushed by him. He watched Cally throw his things into a pack and run to the mule's stall.

"What's the matter with you, Cally?" Jonas asked.

Cally looked out the door to the street. "I got to get back." He tied the last knot and pulled Juliet's head around. "What do I owe you, Jonas?"

"Forget it, Cally. Why are you in such a hurry? You seen a ghost?"

"I . . . I got to get back." Cally put his hand on the big man's sleeve for a second. "You've been good to me, Jonas. I sure thank you."

Jonas growled in his throat. He moved, blocking the way. "You haven't even bought your grub at the store."

"There's no time. Get out of my way, Jonas!" Cally pushed him.

Jonas shook his head. Although Cally argued, he took the little man to the room behind the stable. He filled a sack with flour, sugar, and bacon. "And here's a box of shells for your rifle." He shoved the shells into the sack.

Cally ran back to Juliet. Jonas followed and tied the sack onto the saddle. Fumbling in his pocket, Cally brought out a handful of coins. He put them into Jonas's hand.

The big man stared, then threw the coins down angrily. "You're a stupid, old desert rat, Cally!"

Cally said nothing. He just yanked on the lead rope, turned, and ran with the mule trailing behind. He did stop at the doorway to wave, but then he broke into a run.

He made a wide circle to the south. He looked back once to see Jonas still standing in the doorway, shading his eyes. One day he would like to come back and tell Jonas. . . .

A short ways from town, Cally stopped to let Juliet drink from a creek. He got down on his belly for a drink, too. Then he filled his canteen and took one last look back at the town.

"That was trouble," he said to the old mule. Then he pulled on her rope and started up into the hills.

By late afternoon, Cally was back in his

own country. He began to feel more at ease. He pulled out his pipe and opened the tobacco pouch. It was empty. He shook his head and put the pipe away sadly.

Below him the desert stretched away. He looked back the way he had come. That was when he saw the dust cloud. It was far to the left, where the town of Red Rock was. It was a small cloud that seemed to hang in the air. He was being followed.

Shaking with fear, Cally grabbed the mule's rope and gave it a hard pull.

"It's trouble all right, old girl."

Juliet just swished her tail and started into a walk behind him.

When night fell, Cally stopped to take cover by some rocks. He let Juliet chew on a patch of desert grass. Then he ate a cold supper, pulled out his pipe, and put it away again. He slept badly for two hours, then got up and started on his way. He climbed higher and higher into the mountains. He knew this country, even in the dark.

Toward morning he slept again. Then he got up and went on an hour after sunup. He was very careful to hide his trail.

After crossing the high desert, he looked back. The dust cloud was still there on the horizon. He remembered then that he had told Deputy Fraser just about where the claim was. He would have to go to the cabin, pack up what he owned, and leave quickly. He would find another claim . . . somewhere. He chewed on the pipe as he thought. Maybe he should go on to Mexico. He would have no trouble losing himslf south of the Rio Grande. But he hated to give up the claim. He and old Bill had worked so hard on it, and in a few years it might amount to something. At least, old Bill had thought it would.

Cally crossed the last hills. He was almost there. Only a half day's ride was between him and his claim. He made camp again and fell asleep at once.

By noon the next day, his shack was in sight.

He and Juliet came up the narrow valley at a slow walk. There were no tracks at all in the sand. Everything seemed just as he had left it. The old wooden shack leaned quietly against the brown rocks. The mine entrance, a hundred yards up the side of the hill, looked the same as always. Cally tied Juliet in the shade. Then he went one last time into his shack.

He really hated to leave. He was slow getting his things together. He had a hard time deciding what to take and what to leave behind. Old Bill had collected a lot of junk.

Then he heard the sound of a horse outside. Someone had come up the canyon! Cally stood by the door, not knowing what to do.

"**A**ll right, Enright," a hard voice called. "Come on out!"

Cally's heart sank as he looked through the doorway. The man on the horse was Sheriff Roy Thomas. Cally shrank back. "What do you want, Sheriff?"

Thomas stopped his horse a dozen feet from the door and got down. He had a gun in his hand. "Come on out, Cally. Your rifle's over on the mule."

Cally shouted, "I never did anything to you, Sheriff!"

A shot answered him. The bullet tore a chunk from the door, and Cally ducked.

"You know me," the sheriff called. "I saw it that day in the office. You know me from somewhere. I've got to shut your mouth."

"I don't know you. It was the will."

The sheriff's voice was puzzled. "What do you mean?"

Cally made his way to the back of the shack. He looked around for something—anything. "It was the will I was bringing you to make legal," he shouted out to the sheriff. Then, down on the floor of the shack, he saw old Bill's pack. What was it Bill had said? His half of the claim and his gun!

Thomas's voice was angry. "What's a will got to do with anything? Come on out here, Cally, or I'm coming in after you!"

Cally fumbled through the pack and found the gun. It was a big, shiny six-shooter. He pulled it out. The feel of the cold steel made him think that he had a chance. Carefully, he watched the door.

He heard the sheriff's boots on the sand. The sheriff was going to kill him to keep his mouth shut. Cally dropped to the floor. He saw the point of the sheriff's gun in the doorway.

"Time's up," Thomas said in a cold voice.

Then he was standing there in the doorway. His eyes searched the darkness.

Cally raised his gun. His move made the sheriff fire, and the roar of the gunshot bounced off the walls of the little room. But the bullet missed.

Then Cally fired once, and again—and again. The booming sounds left his ears ringing. Smoke from old Bill's gun filled the room.

The doorway was empty.

Suddenly the air was very still. Cally waited a moment before he dared to get to his feet. He saw the toe of a boot just outside the door. Roy Thomas lay there, face down in the dirt. Cally knew at once that the sheriff was dead. He dropped the gun and sank to the ground. For a long time he stared at the body, not able to believe it.

After a while, he took the folded paper from his pocket. Bill Waite's will. He turned it over. On the back side the words "Wanted for Murder" were printed in heavy, black letters. The face of the sheriff, with the scar and the thick, black eyebrows, frowned out at him from the poster. Under the picture was printed "Roy Tobin, alias Roy Taggart." In Red Rock he had called himself Roy Thomas.

Cally sighed and let the will fall from his fingers. He was tired and hungry, shaking from fear. There was a sack of tobacco in the sheriff's shirt pocket. He reached for it and slowly filled his pipe.

Today he needed to rest. Tomorrow he would have to start back to Red Rock with the poster and Roy Tobin's body.